I0459132

DENISE FRENETTE

MORE...

Because It's Time

AN INVITATION TO A WORLD OF TRANSFORMATION

Copyright © 2025 Denise Frenette

Published by Lucky Book Publishing: www.luckybookpublishing.com

All rights reserved. No part of this book may be reproduced or used in any manner without the prior written permission of the copyright owner, except for the use of brief quotations in a book review.

The author does not dispense medical advice or prescribe the use of any technique as a form of treatment for physical, emotional, or medical problems without the advice of a physician, either directly or indirectly. The intent of the author is only to offer information of a generally true nature to help you in your quest for emotional, physical, and spiritual well-being. In the event you use any of the information in this book for yourself, the author and the publisher assume no responsibility for your actions.

To request permissions, contact the publisher at hello@luckybookpublishing.com.

Paperback ISBN: 978-1-97775-46-1
Hardcover ISBN: 978-1-97775-45-4
E-book ISBN: 978-1-97775-44-7

https://www.denisefrenette.com/book

First edition, December 2025

DEDICATION ♥

This is my first book, and I was told I need to write a dedication. Well, this ended up being harder than I thought!

My first instinct was definitely to dedicate my book to my son **Kevin**, because his birth changed my life forever. He introduced me to so much *MORE* without even knowing it. That kind of love? No words…

And then I thought, what about my husband, **John**? His support has been absolutely unmatched!

And then my thoughts went to my stepdaughter, **Cheyenne**, who has brought so many new and beautiful experiences to my life.

And then? My sisters, my brothers... Well, you get the idea.

So, with all of that shared,

I've decided to dedicate this book to **MORE** itself and all that it represents to **YOU**, the reader.

WHAT YOU'LL DISCOVER

HI, IT'S ME, DENISE

Before you dive in, I just wanted to say hey. Thanks for showing up. Thanks for being curious enough to pick this up, brave enough to open it up, and generous enough to give me some of your time.

I'm about to share some pretty raw pieces of my story with you: the messy, the magical, and everything in between. My hope? That somewhere in these pages, you'll recognize yourself. Not my life, but your own untold story of wanting *more*, deserving *more*, and finally claiming it.

So grab whatever makes you feel at home, coffee, wine, tea, or, hell, even water if you're fancy like that, and let's talk. Because what we're about to explore together? It's not really about me at all.

It's about **you**. And the *MORE* that's been waiting for you your whole life.

PART 1: WHY

WHY DO WE NEED *MORE?*

Moment of Realization

I have days of despair, and I also have days filled with so much hope and love.

The dark days bring raw awareness of the need that surrounds us all. The days of hope and love bring solutions to the brokenness and the healing of hearts. I am grateful for both: the awakening of despair and the rising of hope.

WITH THAT SAID, I WELCOME YOU TO... DISCOVERING THE BEAUTY, POWER, AND ESSENTIAL BEING OF MORE.

I've spent the last four years searching for the right words to make you feel what I feel, to see the world the way I've come to see it. And honestly? I'm still not sure I'll ever find the perfect way to say it. But here's what I know for certain: this book needed to be written.

Because for so long, I struggled with the idea of wanting *more*. The guilt. The confusion. The ache. Maybe you have too.

I used to think that wanting *more* meant I was ungrateful. Ungrateful for the beauty and abundance that surrounded me. That it made me selfish, or greedy, or somehow wrong for daring to ask for something beyond what I already had. How can it be okay for me to want *more* while others are dying of hunger or in need of housing, and when there's a world in need of so much!

I carried that guilt like a weight, until one day, it occurred to me that wanting less never fixed anything. It only made me smaller. And when we limit ourselves, our wants, and ignore who we are, we lose curiosity, courage, and the boldness to invent new ways forward.

PUTTING LIMITS ON OUR HOPES DOESN'T BRING HELP TO OTHERS. IT BRINGS MORE LIMITATIONS.

That realization gave me permission to see the world differently: through a lens of hope, of vision, of *more*. Not just for myself, but for all of us. Because when we allow ourselves to want *more*, we're not just dreaming; we're creating.

WANTING MORE ISN'T A
BETRAYAL OF WHAT YOU
HAVE. IT'S A CELEBRATION
OF WHAT'S POSSIBLE.

—Denise Frenette

I now understand that my guilt about wanting *more* wasn't helping anyone. Not the hungry. Not the homeless. Not the suffering. My smallness didn't feed a single person or house a single family.

But you know what does help?
People who expand their capacity. People
who refuse to play small. People who
build something meaningful and then
reach back to pull others up with them.

Waris Dirie (Somalia/Austria) – Escaped an arranged marriage at 13, became a refugee, worked as a house servant, then as a janitor at McDonald's. Eventually became a supermodel and UN ambassador, but *more* importantly, founded the Desert Flower Foundation to combat female genital mutilation. She transformed her own suffering into a global movement that has helped millions of girls.

Kiran Mazumdar-Shaw (India) – Started Biocon in her garage in 1978 with about $200. As a woman in India's male-dominated business world, she faced constant rejection from banks and investors. Now she runs India's largest biopharmaceutical company, employs thousands, and makes life-saving medications affordable for developing countries.

Ingvar Kamprad (Sweden) – Grew up in rural poverty and started selling matches door-to-door as a child. Founded IKEA with the vision that good design shouldn't be only for the wealthy. His *more* literally democratized furniture design, making functional, beautiful homes accessible to millions of low-income families worldwide.

Leymah Gbowee (Liberia) – A teenage mother escaping domestic violence who became a social worker. She organized the women's peace movement that ended Liberia's brutal civil war. Won the Nobel Peace Prize. Her expansion from survival mode to activist didn't take from others; it brought peace to an entire nation.

José Mujica (Uruguay) – Spent 14 years in prison, two of them at the bottom of a well. Became the president of Uruguay and donated 90% of his salary to charity, living simply on his farm. His *more* wasn't material. It was expanding what's possible in political leadership and proving that leaders can serve without enriching themselves.

Howard Schultz (USA) – Founder of Starbucks, grew up in Brooklyn public housing, watching his father struggle after a work injury with no health insurance. He could have carried guilt about wanting *more*. Instead, he built

Starbucks and made it the first company to offer comprehensive health benefits and stock options to part-time workers. His *more* created benefits for hundreds of thousands of employees.

And **Dolly Parton (USA)** – Born in a one-room cabin in rural Tennessee, one of twelve children in dire poverty. She's now created the Imagination Library, which has given over 200 million free books to children. Her expansion didn't take from others; it created a literacy program that reaches children in poverty across multiple countries.

Think about it this way: a doctor who limits herself, who stays comfortable, who never pushes for *more* knowledge, *more* skills, *more* impact—she helps fewer people. But the doctor who demands *more* of herself, who expands her capacity, who builds a practice or trains other doctors or innovates new treatments? She multiplies her impact exponentially.

That's what *More* actually does. It doesn't limit others. It expands what's possible for everyone.

Now, I know what you might be thinking: "Denise, those are incredible people. But I'm not Dolly Parton. I'm not going to win a Nobel Prize or build a billion-dollar company. And honestly? I thought this book was going to be about manifesting *more* in my *own* life, the dream vacation, the financial freedom, the joy I've been craving. Does my personal *more* even matter if I'm not changing the world?"

And here's what I need you to hear: **Yes. Absolutely yes.**

Your *more* gets to be both/and, not either/or. The dream vacation you're craving? The financial freedom? The joy? Those aren't selfish wants that somehow cancel out your ability to make a difference. They're part of your expansion. And your expansion, whether it looks like world-changing impact or personal fulfillment, **it all matters.**

Because changing the world isn't reserved for the famous or the exceptional. It happens in the quiet moments, too. In the small acts of kindness that ripple out in ways we'll never fully see.

It's the teacher who stays late to help a struggling student, not knowing that encouragement will be the turning point in that child's life.

It's the neighbor who checks on the elderly woman next door, whose presence becomes the only human connection she has all week.

It's the parent who breaks a generational cycle of anger and chooses to speak gently to their child, rewriting the future for generations to come.

It's you, choosing to smile at a stranger who's having the worst day of their life, and that smile becomes the reason they don't give up.

Your growth, your creativity, your efforts don't always get measured. They won't always be recognized. There's no Forbes list for the mother who raises emotionally healthy children, no awards ceremony for the friend who listens without judgment, no headline for the person who simply chooses to be kinder today than they were yesterday.

But that doesn't make your *more* any less powerful. Sometimes the most profound changes happen in the invisible spaces between people. In the moments no one's watching. In the decisions that seem small but shift everything.

So don't let these big examples discourage you. Let them inspire you to see that you being you, quirks and all, matters. Your *"more"* doesn't have to look like anyone else's. It just has to be authentically yours.

> **When we shrink ourselves out of guilt, we're not being humble. We're withholding our gifts. We're refusing to become the people who have the resources, the influence, the capacity to actually make a difference.**

Because when you choose *more* kindness, *more* courage, *more* authenticity, *more* forgiveness, *more* love, *more* exciting experiences, you're not just changing your life. You're changing the lives of everyone you touch. And they'll touch others. And those ripples? They never stop.

When we allow ourselves to want *more*, we're not just dreaming. We're creating.

"*MORE* ISN'T SOMETHING YOU CHASE; IT'S SOMETHING YOU BECOME WHEN YOU START SEEING YOUR BEAUTY AND WORTH."

– Denise Frenette

Every morning, I have this ritual. I listen to motivational "Christian" music. My husband used to groan, "Again?!" But now? Now he gets it. I'm not a religious person, but there's something about certain songs that stirs my soul. And one day, a particular song stopped me in my tracks.

I was in my kitchen, coffee mug in hand, probably still in my pajamas, when the opening chords hit. It's a song about demanding *more, more* from life, from God, from ourselves. The beat was electric, and the lyrics? Well, they wrecked me. I'd listen and cry, not because I didn't want *more*, but because I did. Because every word felt like it was being sung directly to the little girl inside me who had learned to make herself smaller, quieter, molded into what was expected.

I must have played that song twenty times that first day. My husband walked through the kitchen and just shook his head, probably thinking I'd lost my mind.

BUT I HADN'T LOST IT.
I WAS FINDING IT.

Growing up in a strict Catholic household, I was taught to be grateful, to accept. On the outside, we were the perfect family: six kids, my mother the church organ player, my father the respected businessman. We sat in the front pew every Sunday, dressed like little saints. People admired us. Some even envied us.

But behind closed doors? It was a different story.

As you read through these pages and discover *more*, one of the things I hope you capture is that *more* doesn't ask you to pretend. It doesn't care about appearances. It just asks: "What if there's another way? What if there is *more*? *More* safety, *more* love, *more* hope, *more* answers?"

THE TURNING POINT

One day, I decided I was done struggling with the idea of *more*.

Done feeling guilty for wanting.

Done apologizing for dreaming.

I WAS DONE.

And that's when it hit me.

More isn't just a desire. It's a force.

It's beautiful. Powerful. Magical.

It's the key. One that unlocks doors we didn't even know were closed.

WHY THIS BOOK?

I'm not here to give you a perfectly packaged, step-by-step guide. Life isn't like that, and neither is *more*.

This book is a conversation. The kind we'd have over coffee, leaning in close, laughing, maybe even crying a little. It's messy. It's honest. It's real.

It's my life, and I want it to be yours as well.

As I write this book, my hope isn't just to share my story. It's to ignite yours. To make you believe, deep in your being, that *more* isn't just possible.

It's necessary.

SO, WITH THAT SAID, LET'S BEGIN.

I WANT *MORE*

More love
More clarity
More freedom
More courage
More solutions
More sharing
More kindness
More understanding
More unity
More insight
More awareness
More peace
More laughter
More impact

More abundance... and yes, that definitely includes *more* money, and *more* 5-star restaurants! (Yes, I'm a foodie.)

I know! That's a lot! And I want to share with you how and why this came about.

"HOPE ISN'T SOMETHING THAT JUST SIMPLY APPEARS. IT'S SOMETHING YOU CREATE WITH EVERY SMALL, BRAVE CHOICE YOU MAKE."

— *Denise Frenette*

THE TRUTH

Every story has layers, and the truth depends on who's telling it.

Truth is not a fixed point. It is a reflection, shaped by where we stand, what we've lived, and what we fear or hope for. The same moment can be a wound, a triumph, or a prison, depending on who tells the story.

What I'm about to share with you is the same story told three different ways, each version completely true, each version revealing something different about the nature of pain, love, and the complex inheritance we pass down through generations.

LET ME TELL YOU ABOUT A MAN.

Version One: The Boy

Once, he was small. The house was loud, not with laughter, but with want. His father's voice was a storm, unpredictable, leaving bruises on skin and spirit. He watched his father drink, angry at a world that didn't allow him to put enough food on the table. His mother's eyes were always tired, her hands too weak to shield him. Fear and consequence were his daily companions, as sure as the sun rises and sets. He felt alone, scared, and hopelessness became a way of life. He learned early: powerlessness is a kind of hunger. It stripped him of vision and slowly created a loneliness filled with anger.

So he made a promise to the dark: *I will never be like him.*

And another, quieter vow: I will never be ignored and powerless again.

Version Two: The Man

Decades later, he stands tall in a suit that costs more than his childhood home. Awards line his office walls. His wife wears pearls; his children have three meals a day, a good roof over their heads, and a home to be proud of. He teaches them the importance of hard work because he knows what happens when lack and inconsistency are part of life. He works late, not just for the money, but for the certainty it brings. He teaches them that discipline is love. That rules are safety, because he knows the cost of chaos.

When his son spills juice on the polished table, his voice sharpens. "Pay attention!" The child flinches. For a heartbeat, the man hesitates, but no. Better this fear than the kind he grew up with. Better this pain than the humiliation of lack. He is not his father. He provides. That is love. Isn't it?

Version Three: The Son

The boy is seven. His father is a giant, a god who brings presents and punishments with the same stern hands. He tries to memorize the rules: Don't laugh too loud. Don't cry. Don't fail. But his knees are always scraped, his homework smudged.

At night, he presses his face into the pillow so no one hears him sob. His mother kisses his forehead, but her hands shake when his father shouts. The boy loves him. Hates him. Wants to be him. Wonders why he's never enough for him.

"NOTHING IN LIFE IS TO BE FEARED, IT IS ONLY TO BE UNDERSTOOD. NOW IS THE TIME TO UNDERSTAND MORE, SO THAT WE MAY FEAR LESS."

— *Marie Curie*

THE MIRROR

Three truths. Three versions.

The boy who swore not to become his father now terrifies his own child. The provider who measures love in sacrifice leaves bruises he doesn't see. The son who aches will one day grow up and decide, in his own way, what not to be.

Where is the truth here? In the wound?
The intention? The consequence?

It is in all of them. And none of them.

I've learned that the truth shifts when we dare to look through another's eyes. And that shift is where compassion begins. Where solutions are found. Where old stories can be rewritten. Where a man might, if he lets himself, see his son's tears and remember the boy he once was. And change.

As I look back and reflect, I now understand that flexibility of perception is the key to *more*. *More* understanding. *More* healing. *More* futures unshackled from the past.

I now know that the question isn't "What is true?" but "Whose truth have I not yet considered?"

Ask it often enough, and you might just find a deeper truth, one that sets you free.

THE SHAME

Because some wounds are too deep to ignore, and healing begins with truth.

Shame is a lie dressed as truth. It tells you that you are broken, that your mistakes define you, that you are unworthy of love. But shame is only a story, one that can be rewritten.

THE MOMENT

I was seven. The house was full: six children, a mother who never stopped moving, a father who demanded perfection. We looked like the ideal family from the outside: church every Sunday, polished shoes, matching dresses. But inside, fear was the unspoken rule.

That morning, I woke up early, heart pounding with hope. The cereal box! The one with the prize inside was sitting on the counter. Oh, how I needed that little plastic treasure, not because it was valuable, but because it was mine. Not a hand-me-down. Not shared. Mine.

But my brother got there first. Again.

The injustice burned. And in that moment, something small and desperate inside me snapped. I marched upstairs, climbed onto my parents' bed, and woke my father with a lie: "He called me a bitch."

I didn't even fully understand the word. But I knew it was bad. Bad enough to punish him. Bad enough to make things fair.

THE CONSEQUENCE

My father took my hand, led me to the kitchen, and called my brother down.

"Did you say this?"

"No," my brother whispered.

But truth didn't matter. Only punishment did.

My father's response was swift and violent. I was made to watch as punishment was delivered, the kind that left marks on the body and scars on the soul.

Something inside me shattered.

This was my fault.

The shame swallowed me whole. Not just for the lie, but for the helplessness, the cruelty, the knowing that I had caused this. That I was part of a cycle I hated but didn't yet understand.

THE NEW LENS

Now, as an adult, I see that moment differently.

THE SHAME WASN'T MINE TO CARRY.

A child who lies to get a prize isn't evil. She's hungry, for fairness, for attention, for something to call her own. The real tragedy wasn't my lie. It was the system that taught my father that love came with conditions, that mistakes meant pain, that worth had to be earned through suffering.

With that said, I also want you to know that **my father wasn't a monster**. He was a man who had been taught the same lessons, harsher, crueler versions of them. His rage wasn't his alone; it was inherited, passed down like an heirloom no one wanted.

WHEN SHAME IS KEPT WITHIN

But here's what I didn't know back then, what took me decades to understand: shame has a way of settling in. It doesn't just visit. It moves in, unpacks its bags, rearranges your furniture. And if you let it stay too long, it becomes the lens through which you see everything.

When you live in shame, you don't just carry guilt about one moment. You start believing you ARE the moment. That lie I told? For years, it became my identity. I was the girl who got her brother beaten. The girl who couldn't be trusted. The girl who ruined everything she touched. And as an adult? Every mistake, every misperceived failure, was just another confirmation of what I *knew to be true*.

Shame convinced me that I was fundamentally broken. And broken things, I believed, didn't deserve beauty. Didn't deserve love. Didn't deserve *more*.

THE PRICE OF STAYING IN THE DARK

What shame does — and this is its cruelest trick — is blur everything. It distorts your memory. It takes the complicated, messy truth of real life and tries to flatten it into something simpler. Something easier to carry.

But life isn't simple. People aren't simple.

When you live in shame, you lose the ability to see clearly. You can't process your experiences with the wisdom and perspective you need to heal. You stay stuck in the confusion of a child who didn't have the tools to understand what was happening.

THE FORGIVENESS WE DENY OURSELVES

Here's what I've learned about forgiveness: it's not about saying what happened was okay. It's not about excusing harm or pretending that love makes violence acceptable.

A crucial part of forgiveness is understanding that someone was doing the best they could with the tools they were given, and also knowing that their best wasn't good enough. Both things are true.

Growing up, my father wasn't always angry. There were mornings he'd make us laugh at breakfast. Afternoons when he'd pull me onto his lap during Saturday cartoons, and I'd feel completely safe. Moments when his eyes would light up talking about his dreams, and I could see the boy he once was: hopeful, full of possibility. He worked hard, and he was proud of his accomplishments. We went on these incredible family trips, and he truly did everything he could to give us a better life than what he experienced as a child. And he did. But, his trauma was never properly acknowledged, and the dysfunctional patterns never fully understood, and thus, unfortunately, they repeated.

As a little girl, I thought the eggshells we walked on were normal. Every family had rules, right? Every dad got *mad* sometimes. And in between the explosions, there was love. I could feel it in his hugs, see it in the way he'd ruffle my hair, hear it in his laugh when something genuinely delighted him. You can imagine the confusion that caused. As a child, I didn't have the emotional capacity to know the difference between love and dysfunction. I didn't understand that you could feel genuine affection from someone who was also genuinely harming you. That both experiences could be real, and one didn't cancel out the other.

As an adult, I now know what was wrong.

THE VIOLENCE WAS WRONG.

The underlying presence of fear was wrong.

The unpredictability that kept us all walking on eggshells was wrong.

Love doesn't terrorize. Love doesn't teach through pain. Love doesn't make children responsible for managing an adult's emotions.

But with that clarity also comes another understanding: my father was trying to love us. He did struggle with how to show it. His view of caring had been so jaded by his own upbringing that tenderness and violence were tangled together in his mind. He genuinely believed that discipline through fear was protection. That providing material things meant he was succeeding. That his children's terror meant they'd be prepared for a harsh world.

HE WAS WRONG.

And here's where forgiveness comes in, not as acceptance of what happened, but as a refusal to let shame write the rest of the story.

Forgiveness allowed me to see the full picture: the hurt boy who became a hurtful man. That same hurt boy who put himself through school and became a successful businessman who was able to provide for a family. The father who loved us in the only broken way he knew how. The violence that was absolutely, unequivocally wrong. The moments of genuine connection that were also real.

SHAME WANTED ME TO CHOOSE ONE TRUTH AND DENY THE OTHER. BUT HEALING DEMANDED THAT I HOLD BOTH.

But let me be crystal clear about something: true, healthy forgiveness only comes with honest acknowledgment.

You have to acknowledge what was wrong.

Name it.

Say it out loud.

**The violence was wrong.
The fear was wrong. The harm was real.**

Understanding that hurt people hurt people doesn't replace the fact that people who cause harm must be held accountable. It doesn't mean they get a free pass. It doesn't mean you stay in dangerous situations waiting for them to heal.

If someone is actively harming you—physically, emotionally, psychologically—they need to be separated from the situation. Removed from access to cause more damage. Not as punishment, but as protection. Protection for you, and honestly, protection for them too, because continuing to harm others only deepens their own wounds.

True healing can only happen when the harm stops. When there's safety. When there's space.

Forgiveness is something you can work toward once you're safe. **But safety comes first. Always.**

When I finally opened myself to the full dimensions of forgiveness, I discovered something profound: I could grieve what never was. I could see my father as *more* than his fears, *more* than his dysfunction, *more* than the man who shaped my childhood pain. I could see the person he was trying to be. The boy he'd been. The dreams he'd carried and lost. This clarity came mostly after he was gone. When the reminders of our shared history finally quieted enough for me to understand. I could only hold space for his brokenness alongside his capacity for love once he was no longer here to trigger my wounds. That's not a coincidence. That's how healing works.

YOU CAN'T HEAL IN THE FIRE. YOU HAVE TO GET OUT FIRST.

So, if you're reading this and thinking about someone who's hurting you right now, please hear me: This book is not asking you to forgive your way through active abuse. It's not asking you to understand someone's pain while they're still inflicting it on you. It's not asking you to be *more* compassionate when you're not safe.

Get safe first. Then, when you're ready, when you're strong, when you're supported — that's when you can choose whether forgiveness serves your healing.

Because when you can finally see clearly and when you can say, "What he did was harmful AND he was doing his best AND his best wasn't enough AND I can still choose not to carry his pain forward," that's when you stop being stuck in shame's blur.

That's when you start living in the clarity of *More*.

Forgiveness says: "What happened was real. The pain was real. And I am choosing not to let it define every moment that comes after."

But here's the thing most people don't tell you about forgiveness: it has to start with yourself. Because if you can't forgive yourself for being imperfect, for making mistakes, for being human, you'll never truly forgive anyone else either.

For years, I held onto my shame like it was proof of my conscience. Like if I just felt bad enough, long enough, I could somehow undo what I'd done. I convinced myself that my suffering was noble. That it meant I cared.

But shame isn't conscience. Conscience says, "I made a mistake and I can learn from it." Shame says, "I AM a mistake and there's no hope for me." One leads to growth. The other leads to paralysis.

THE BEAUTY SHAME HIDES

When you're drowning in shame, you can't see your own beauty. You literally can't. Your brain won't let you. Because if you're fundamentally bad, fundamentally broken, then any evidence to the contrary must be a lie, a fluke, a mistake.

I remember the first time someone told me I was gifted, that my ability to sense energy and connect with the spiritual realm was a treasure. I physically recoiled.

Shame had convinced me that anything good in me was either fake or would eventually be tainted by my brokenness.

But here's the truth that took me decades to accept: my gifts didn't exist in spite of my shame. They existed alongside it. My capacity for deep empathy wasn't separate from my capacity for mistakes. My intuition wasn't proof that I was secretly good underneath. It was just... part of me. Just like the lie I told was part of me. Just like the love I have for my family is part of me.

We are not one thing. We are everything, all at once.

THE LIGHT THAT'S ALWAYS BEEN THERE

My father had serious issues with anger. With unresolved sadness. He was hurt in ways I'll never fully understand. The boy who promised himself he'd never be powerless again became a man who wielded power like a weapon.

But he also had love in his heart.

I remember moments. Love. Real warmth. A tenderness that seemed to surprise even him, like he'd stumbled upon a part of himself he'd forgotten existed.

I believe, with everything in me, that he loved us the best way he could. And that love? It was broken. The head games, the violence, the fear he instilled in us—it was wrong. And it caused damage that ripples through our family still.

But if I stay in the shame, in the fear, mine or his, I can never hold both truths. I can never see him as the hurt boy AND the harmful man. I can never forgive myself for being the child who made a terrible choice AND the woman who has spent her life learning to choose differently.

CHOOSING THE LIGHT

When we stay in the dark too long, in the shame, in the anger, in the story that we or others are beyond redemption, we lose sight of what the light reveals.

The light doesn't erase the darkness. It doesn't pretend the wounds weren't real or the harm didn't happen. But it shows us something shame never can: options.

Options to grow. To change. To choose grace over judgment. To see that forgiveness isn't weakness. It's the bravest damn thing we can do.

Choosing to forgive (myself, my father, the broken systems that shaped us both) didn't mean saying what happened was okay. It meant saying: "I refuse to let this pain be the only story. I refuse to let shame steal my *More*."

Because here's what I know now: holding onto shame isn't protection. It's not proof of your goodness or your conscience. It's just another way we make ourselves small. Another way we accept less than we deserve.

THE GRACE THAT CHANGES EVERYTHING

Grace says: "You were hurt. And in your hurt, you hurt others. And that's the most human thing in the world."

Grace says: "Your father was both the boy who was beaten and the man who beat. And so the cycle continues until someone chooses to see the whole truth."

Grace says: "You can acknowledge the harm AND the love. You can honor the pain AND forgive. You can remember the darkness AND still choose to walk toward the light."

This is what allows us to have *More*. Not the pretending. Not the toxic positivity that says, "Just choose joy!" while ignoring real pain, but the mature, nuanced understanding that humans are complicated. That we are all doing the best we can with what we were given. And that sometimes, the best we can is still not enough, and that's okay.

It's okay to say: "My father's best wasn't enough to keep us safe. And I still love him. And I still grieve what we all lost."

It's okay to say: "I made terrible choices as a child. And I was still just a child. And I can forgive that little girl now."

BOTH THINGS CAN BE TRUE.

THE NAVIGATION

As we navigate both worlds, light and dark, love and harm, beauty and brokenness, we get to choose how long we stay in each place.

Shame wants us to build a home in the dark. To believe that's where we belong. To accept that as our permanent address.

But *More* invites us into the light. Not to live there perfectly, not to pretend the shadows don't exist, but to remember that we have a choice. **Every single day, we get to choose which truth we're nurturing.** Which story we're feeding.

> **Are we feeding the story that says we're broken beyond repair? Or are we feeding the story that says we're beautifully, painfully, gloriously human, capable of both harm and healing?**

THE MORE

What was needed that day?

More **love.** The kind that doesn't demand perfection.

More **protection.** For my siblings. For me. For my father, who never had it.

More **understanding.** Of why a child lies. Of why a man hurts.

More **forgiveness.** For myself. For him.

More **solutions.** Instead of punishment, curiosity. Why did you do that? What did you need?

More **kindness.** For the little girl who just wanted to matter. For the man who thought cruelty was discipline.

And *more* **grace**, the kind that says, "You are allowed to be imperfect. You are allowed to have been hurt and to have caused hurt. You are allowed to learn. You are allowed to change. You are allowed to choose differently now."

THE CHOICE

My father is gone now. I speak to his spirit sometimes, not the angry man, but the boy he once was. The one who wanted to be loved. The one who tried, in his broken way, to give us what he thought we needed.

I choose to see that version of him.

Not because the other version wasn't real. But because I refuse to let shame, his or mine, be the end of the story.

Because shame only survives in the dark. When we bring it into the light, when we ask, "What was really happening here?", it loses its power.

Shame says, "You are bad."

But the truth is: "You were hurt. And hurt people hurt people. And you can choose not to pass that hurt forward."

The way out isn't through carrying the weight of shame. It's through MORE.

More compassion.

More curiosity.

More rewriting of the stories that keep us small.

More understanding that perfection was never the goal. Wholeness was.

> **Shame is an illusion. And love, the kind that understands, forgives, and heals, is the only truth that lasts.**

THE CASE FOR MORE

BECAUSE SETTLING ISN'T HUMILITY. IT'S SURRENDER.

We are taught to be satisfied. To be grateful for what we have, and we should be. But gratitude is not the enemy of desire. In fact, the deepest gratitude demands that we ask for *more*, not just for ourselves, but for everyone.

BECAUSE *MORE* IS NOT GREED. IT IS EVOLUTION.

THE LENS THAT CHANGES EVERYTHING

Here's what I've come to understand: the same limitation that kept me from claiming my own beauty, the belief that I couldn't be worthy if I'd also caused harm, that I couldn't deserve joy while carrying shame, shows up everywhere. In how we see ourselves, how we relate to others, and how we engage with the world around us.

IT'S THE SAME PATTERN, JUST
ON DIFFERENT SCALES.

For years, I saw things in absolutes. Either I acknowledged the suffering, the wars, the violence, the systematic destruction of entire communities in the name of religion, politics, or old wounds, or I allowed myself to experience beauty and joy. But never both. As if enjoying a five-star meal somehow negated the hungry. As if experiencing love meant I was turning my back on those being harmed.

But once I came to terms with the complexity of my father, once I learned I could love parts of him without accepting that anger and violence are acceptable, once I could forgive the wounded boy while still condemning the harm he caused, everything shifted.

That same flexibility allowed me to view the world differently.

I realized I'd been looking away from suffering because facing it felt like it would steal my joy. I'd been numbing myself because I didn't know how to feel pain without being consumed by it. I couldn't hold complexity in the world because I hadn't learned to hold it within myself first.

But what if the opposite is true? What if our ability to see and hold both light and dark, in ourselves and in the world, is exactly what's needed? Not one or the other. Both. Always both.

"WE CAN DISAGREE AND
STILL LOVE EACH OTHER
UNLESS YOUR
DISAGREEMENT IS ROOTED
IN MY OPPRESSION AND
DENIAL OF MY HUMANITY
AND RIGHT TO EXIST."

— *James Baldwin*

THE HUNGER THAT BUILT THE WORLD

Every great leap in human history began with a refusal to accept "enough."

The first person who imagined *more* than survival built a home.

The first person who wanted *more* than silence created music.

The first person who demanded *more* justice changed laws.

We call this ambition, vision, or faith. But, at its core, it is simply the refusal to believe that suffering is inevitable. That lack is permanent. That the way things are is the way they must always be.

Let me give you a personal example. A client of mine worked tirelessly to keep her family fed and clothed, but she never questioned the system that made it so hard. She accepted struggle as virtue, scarcity as humility. But what if she had dared to want *more*? Not just for herself, but for her family? What if she had believed that a mother's love shouldn't have to choose between putting food on the table and being present for her children's bedtime stories?

44

**That "what if" is why I write. That
"what if" is why this book exists.**

Wanting *more* opportunities, *more* peace, wanting good shelters for the homeless, water for those who thirst, wanting a planet that breathes, is this selfish?

THE LIE OF "ENOUGH"

Society tells us:

- "Be content." But it never asks: "Content with what?"

- "Don't be selfish." But who decided wanting better is selfish?

- "You have so much already." And yet, why does it still not feel like enough?

**Here's the truth: wanting *more* is not
ungratefulness. It is intelligence.**

If a mother looks at her child and thinks, "I want *more* for you," is that greed? No. It is love in motion.

"EVERY TIME YOU CHOOSE
COMPASSION OVER
JUDGMENT, YOU'RE NOT
JUST CHANGING ONE
MOMENT. YOU'RE
REWRITING GENERATIONS."

– Denise Frenette

THE *MORE* THAT CHANGES EVERYTHING

When we say we want *more*, we are not just speaking of accumulation. We are speaking of expansion.

More love does not mean hoarding affection; it means creating so much of it that it spills over to those who have been starved of it.

More money is not just about wealth; it is about the freedom to lift others as you climb.

More understanding is not just knowledge; it is the bridge between "me" and "we."

This is the "why." Because stagnation is not peace. It is slow suffocation. Because the opposite of *more* is not "enough." It is resignation.

I learned this lesson viscerally when I was standing in that kitchen, crying over a song about demanding *more*. For years, I had accepted that my voice didn't matter, that my dreams were selfish, that my gifts were foolish, and that wanting anything beyond survival was ungrateful. I had resigned myself to a smaller life, and it was killing me slowly, one swallowed dream at a time.

The moment I dared to want **more** wasn't rebellion; it was resurrection.

And that's when I understood how the patterns we explored earlier (the truth about my father, the shame I carried) were all connected to this same limitation.

THE STORIES WE CARRY

In *The Truth*, we saw how pain passes through generations when "enough" is never questioned.

In *The Shame*, we saw how cycles repeat when we accept punishment as love.

But what if we dared to want *more*?

What if the boy who swore, "I will never be like him," had also been taught how to break the cycle, not just with discipline, but with tenderness?

What if the father had known that provision is not just money, but presence?

What if the daughter had been shown that her worth was not earned, but inherent?

THIS IS THE "WHY."

BECAUSE THE WORLD CHANGES WHEN WE REFUSE TO ACCEPT INHERITED LIMITATIONS.

THE INVITATION

This book invites you not only to accept the receiving of *more*, but also to embrace the becoming of *more*.

Becoming the kind of people who:

- See scarcity and ask, "How can we create abundance?"

- See pain and ask, "What healing is possible?"

- See division and say, "There is always room for more unity."

The journey begins with a single question: What if *more* is not just possible but necessary? Because the alternative is a world that stays exactly as it is. And that, my friends, is not enough.

Now that we've explored the "why," why *more* isn't selfish but necessary, why our perspectives can transform our pain into purpose, why the stories we inherit don't have to define our future, you might be wondering: "But what does this *more* actually look like? How do I recognize it? How do I know when I'm living in its essence?"

That's exactly where we're going next. Because understanding why we need *more* is just the beginning. The real magic happens when we learn to see it, feel it, and embody it in every moment of our lives.

In the absence of greed, there is **ABUNDANCE**.

In the absence of fear, there is **FAITH**.

In the absence of ignorance, there is **KNOWLEDGE**.

In the absence of darkness, there is **LIGHT**.

In the absence of war, there is **PEACE**.

In the absence of hate, there is **LOVE**.

PART 2: WHAT

WHAT DOES *MORE* ACTUALLY MEAN?

Finding Direction

WHAT DOES IT MEAN TO LIVE IN THE ESSENCE OF MORE?

This is one of the questions that began my journey. I started sifting through memories, examining the moments that left their mark on my soul. Were they tied to possessions? Achievements? Pain? Or were they something else, something deeper?

More is the recognition that we are meant for expansion. For growth, for depth, for a life that thrums with meaning. It's a mindset, a way of moving through the world with open eyes and an open heart. It's the courage to shed the lies we've been fed: that we are not enough, that wanting is shameful, that joy must be earned through suffering.

BUT HERE IS THE SECRET: *More* **is already here.**

It's not just in the grand gestures or rare luxuries, but in the ordinary magic of the present. In the way sunlight spills through the window in the morning. In the laughter of a friend. In the quiet strength that rises when we face a challenge.

What if we chose to see obstacles not as barriers, but as invitations? What if every difficulty is simply the Universe asking us to tilt our heads, to shift our gaze, to discover a new angle we hadn't noticed before?

A closed door is not the end. It's a sign to turn around and see not just the open window, but a multitude of them. A setback is not failure; it's an opportunity to expand our vision, to question our assumptions, to realize that what we thought was the only path was merely one of many.

The same situation can be a prison or a discovery. It all depends on how we choose to see it. *More* is the practice of looking again. Of asking: What beauty have I missed? What possibility is hidden here?

THE SURPRISE THAT CAME WITH *MORE*

Let me tell you a story that will probably make you laugh, cringe, and maybe see your own life a little differently.

A while back, I was done with my marriage. (My second one. The one I'm still in.) I had my husband completely figured out: lazy, negative, holding me back from the life I deserved. I was convinced that if I could just get out, everything would be better. So, like any fed-up woman with a plan, I said, "F*ck it." (Because yes, I do that. I swear.)

I started aligning my ducks. I crunched numbers, mapped out my solo future, even hit the gym so I'd look good for my next relationship. (Don't judge me, I was petty and motivated.) I gave myself six to nine months to bolt.

And while I was at it, I decided to finally own who I was, a Spiritual Synergist (fancy term for "I see energy, spirit, and patterns most people don't"). I'd hidden that part of myself for years, afraid of ridicule, of not being "enough." But now? I was done playing small.

Here's the funny part: I started changing. Not just my body (though yes, endorphins are a hell of a drug), but my mind. My energy. My happiness. And all while still living with the same man I was convinced was the problem.

One day, I caught myself laughing with him. Then wanting to go to dinner with him. Then—gasp—enjoying his company.

But I wasn't about to be fooled by a few good moments. No way. I stayed the course, kept planning my exit. Except... I never left.

Because I had changed. Not him. Me.

Somewhere in my rage-fueled reinvention, I started seeing myself differently. I started seeing him differently. Not as the anchor dragging me down, but as a human—flawed, yes, but also kind, steady, and weirdly supportive in ways I'd been too pissed to notice. And when I shifted, so did our marriage. Not because he transformed into Prince Charming, but because I stopped waiting for him to.

Now? I'm still in love with that man. The same man I was ready to ditch. Because when I chose *More* for myself, *more* honesty, *more* health, *more* self-respect, I stopped needing him to be different to be happy.

But let's be crystal clear: if your partner is abusive (physically, emotionally, or otherwise), get out. Full stop.

More doesn't mean tolerating harm. It means knowing you deserve safety, love, and a life without suffering. Reach out. Find help. You are worth so much *more* than pain.

THE LESSON? *MORE* ISN'T ABOUT PRETENDING EVERYTHING'S FINE. IT'S ABOUT ASKING: "WHAT IF THE CHANGE 'WE' NEED STARTS WITH ME?"

"MY MISSION IN LIFE IS NOT
MERELY TO SURVIVE, BUT
TO THRIVE; AND TO DO SO
WITH SOME PASSION, SOME
COMPASSION, SOME
HUMOR, AND SOME STYLE."

– Maya Angelou

LIVING *MORE* AS A DAILY CHOICE

Through the years, I discovered that living in a world of *More* is a mindset. It is a choice.

This is something I work on every single day. Living in the *more* demands transparency. It asks for a truth that I didn't even know was there. My discovery of *more* came in my depths of pain, struggles, and times of need.

Seeing, accepting, and allowing grace to soothe the brokenness in me, that's what allowed me to start seeing others with eyes of kindness and understanding, which finally allowed me to begin the process of forgiving my father.

And this process? Understanding that he was doing the best he could with the tools he was given, recognizing that the pain he inflicted upon his children was the pain that lived in his soul—this understanding is what introduced me to *more*.

MORE GRACE.

MORE LOVE.

MORE PEACE.

MORE AWARENESS.

When we train ourselves to see this way, the world softens. When your world softens, your morning traffic jam becomes a chance to finally listen to that podcast. Your difficult coworker becomes an opportunity to communicate differently. Your financial stress becomes information, not about your worth, but about what needs to shift. Struggles become indicators. Ordinary moments become extraordinary. The "not enough" transforms into "opportunities," because abundance is all around us; it is the seeing of different perspectives and having the flexibility to shift into a light that brings new hope.

More frees us. It says: You are worthy now. Not when you achieve, not when you acquire, but now, as you are. It is the understanding that love, safety, and beauty are not privileges for the few, but birthrights for all.

More is the past whispering its lessons, the future glowing with possibility, and the present moment alive with both. It is the light we carry within, a light that, when shared, illuminates the world.

SO, ASK YOURSELF: WHAT IS MY *MORE?*

And then, dare to reach for it. But first? Look around. It might already be here, waiting for you to see it.

Now that you understand what *More* truly is, not just a desire but a way of being, not just a destination but a lens, you're probably wondering: "Okay, Denise, this all sounds beautiful, but HOW?"

How do I make this shift from wanting *more* to being *more*?

That's exactly where we're going next. Because understanding *More* is just the beginning. The real transformation happens when you learn the practical steps to embody it daily.

"I AM NO LONGER
ACCEPTING THE THINGS I
CANNOT CHANGE. I AM
CHANGING THE THINGS I
CANNOT ACCEPT."

— *Angela Davis,*
American political activist

PART 3: HOW

HOW DO WE LIVE IN *MORE*?

The Path Forward

THE DAY I STOPPED HIDING (AND STARTED FLYING)

Here's what nobody tells you about wanting *More*: understanding it is the easy part. The hard part? Actually living it.

I spent years knowing I wanted *more* but staying frozen. Terrified of what people would think. Worried I'd fail. Convinced I wasn't ready.

Then one day, I got so fed up with my own excuses that I threw my hands up and said, "Fine, Universe, you take the wheel!"

It wasn't pretty. It wasn't graceful. But damn, was it freeing.

I stopped dimming my light. I stopped censoring myself. I stopped waiting for permission to be who I actually am, intuitive gifts, spiritual weirdness, and all. I built a business around helping people see the patterns keeping them stuck: the energetic blocks, the inherited stories, the soul-level contracts with limitations like "Good girls don't ask for too much" or "Who am I to think I deserve better?"

And you know what? My business didn't crash and burn. It thrived.

But here's the deeper truth: the "how" of *More* isn't about finding the right strategy or technique. It's about finally having the courage to be who you really are. And then? It's about the daily practices that keep you there.

BECAUSE INSIGHT WITHOUT ACTION IS JUST PRETTY PHILOSOPHY.

So let's talk about the actual "how."

THE FOUNDATION: FAITH AS STRATEGY

The first thing that comes to mind when people ask, "How do I get *More*?"

FAITH. And I know it sounds vague and corny, but hear me out.

Faith, the secret they don't teach you in business school, is the "how" of *More*. Not the "cross your fingers" kind of faith. Not wishful thinking. But the kind of faith that says:

- "I don't know how this will work, but I trust it will."

- "Even if I can't see all of the path yet, I'm taking the first step."

- "The Universe/God/Spirit, whatever you call it, has my back."

For me, that meant:

- Praying like it's a strategy meeting. (Because it is. And no, I'm not talking about a "Hail Mary" or "Our Father." I'm talking real conversations.)

- Meditating like it's a download session. (Your intuition is Wi-Fi for divine intel.)

- Playing my hype music like it's a pep talk from the cosmos. (Sometimes the Universe speaks in bass drops.)

And the craziest part? The *more* I leaned into faith, the *more* doors flew open. Not because I "manifested" like a wizard, but because I finally got out of my own damn way.

> **But before we dive into the practical steps, I need to be honest with you about what "living in *More*" actually looks like when life gets hard.**

THE TRUTH ABOUT STRUGGLE

I need you to understand something crucial: living in the essence of *More* does not remove grief. It doesn't negate anger and doesn't remove sadness. And I want to be transparent and honest with you about what "living in *More*" actually looks like when life gets hard.

Living in the essence of *More* allows the tears of anger, pain, defeat, and loneliness to flow through you, alongside tears of grace, love, hope, safety, and freedom. Tears that create space to heal and bring awakenings that only the light of *More* can illuminate.

I want you to understand how important the struggle is. Because the struggle is the part that makes you see the light. The struggle is what makes you understand what *More* truly means. When you see lack, you see *More*.

Let me show you what I mean with a story that nearly broke me, and then remade me completely.

WHEN DARKNESS DEMANDED LIGHT

Before I share this next part of my story, I need you to know something: it gets heavy. Really heavy. But there's light at the end, I promise you that. And *more* importantly, there's a reason I'm taking you through this darkness with me.

Living in the essence of *More* isn't a straight line. It's not a simple "think positive and everything gets better" kind of journey. It's a fluid process that brings awareness you didn't ask for, challenges that break you open, questions that demand you look at everything differently, and, yes, moments of sheer, unexpected beauty that make it all worth it.

This story? It's all of that. The mess, the pain, the discovery, and, eventually, the light. So take a breath. Maybe grab that coffee or tea. And know that we're going somewhere good. We just have to walk through the fire first.

AFTER DISCOVERING THE DEBT

A few days after my father died, we got a big surprise. We found out about his "estate," or the lack thereof. My father had a good career and a great pension that paid for the nice retirement home my parents lived in. But a few days after his death, my siblings, my 86-year-old mother, and I discovered my father was penniless. No more pension, no savings, no life insurance. Nothing. Same for my mother.

They had both gambled it all away. **Addiction had stolen not just their money but their ability to see what they were losing.** There was only debt.

My anger, my shock, and the deep shame I felt once again. Part of me thought: this is the natural consequence of their choices. Another part of me just felt heartbroken.

"FAITH IS THE BIRD THAT SINGS WHILE THE DAWN IS STILL DARK."

— *Rabindranath Tagore, Nobel laureate*

But this wasn't really a surprise, was it? Not if I'm being honest.

A few years before my father retired, he was diagnosed with Parkinson's disease. And I have to tell you something: at first, a small part of me didn't believe him. I thought maybe he was exaggerating. Looking for attention. Being dramatic.

I felt ashamed about that for years. But I don't anymore. Because I now understand that the doubt wasn't mine to carry. It was a survival mechanism born from a childhood of manipulation and mind games. When you've had to walk on eggshells and doubt so much, you learn to question everything, even legitimate medical diagnoses. My disbelief wasn't a character flaw. It was a scar.

And then the disease set in. Really set in. And it was horrible. I would not wish that on anyone.

I watched my father, this strong, controlling, larger-than-life man, start to lose his body. The tremors. The shuffling walk. The way his face became a mask, unable to show the emotions I knew were raging inside him. This man, who'd spent his whole life terrified of being powerless, was now watching his own body betray him.

He changed during those years. Not just physically, but in every way. **The disease progressed relentlessly. And with it, the drinking and gambling, no longer occasional escapes, but daily rituals of avoidance.** He actually softened in some ways, but that softness came with a desperate need to numb what he was facing. Both of them, my mother right alongside him, diving deeper into the bottles and the casinos like they could drown the reality closing in.

I so wanted things to be different. God, how I wanted it. I wanted them to face this with grace, with courage, with the kind of dignity that turns tragedy into something meaningful. I wanted to care for them, to show up, to be the daughter who helped them through this impossible thing.

But they made it so damn difficult.

Every family gathering became overshadowed by their drinking. Birthday parties where we'd have to watch how much wine was poured. Celebrations that should have been about joy, about family, about connection, all of it tainted by the question: How drunk are they going to get today?

My healthy boundaries were constantly tested. Do I show up knowing it's going to be painful? Do I stay away and feel guilty? Do I try to control their drinking and become the bad guy? Do I pretend everything's fine and enable the chaos?

There were no good answers. Just a series of impossible choices that left me exhausted and heartbroken.

And when they retired, everything accelerated. Without the structure of work, without daily responsibilities to anchor them, with the Parkinson's stripping away more control each day—the addiction that had lurked in the shadows moved center stage. All that empty time became a void they tried desperately to fill.

The phone calls started. Late-night calls where I couldn't understand what they were saying. Calls asking for money, just a little bit to get them through. Calls that made my stomach drop because I knew they'd been drinking, and I knew they still had car keys.

And with that also came the hospital visits. My father falling at the casino, drunk, breaking bones. My mother falling at home. The same cycle, over and over. The doctors who would look at us with that expression, the one that said they'd seen this before, and they knew how this story usually ended.

And every time the phone rang late at night, my heart would stop. Were they driving drunk? Had they hurt someone? Hurt themselves? Were they calling from a hospital? Or worse, would it be a hospital calling about them?

It was exhausting. The worry, the anger, the helplessness of watching two people you love destroy themselves in slow motion. Watching them choose the bottle and the slot machines over everything else. Over dignity. Over security. Over us.

Some of my siblings couldn't do it anymore. They distanced themselves. Set boundaries. Stopped answering the calls, stopped showing up to the hospital, stopped trying to save people who didn't want to be saved.

And you know what? I didn't blame them. Not for a second.

They had every right to protect themselves. Every right to say, "I can't watch this anymore." Every right to choose their own peace over the chaos our parents kept creating.

And yet, that distance, those necessary, healthy boundaries, separated us. The family that was already fractured by fear and violence in childhood was now scattered by addiction in their adulthood. Some of us still trying to help, some of us done trying, all of us just trying to survive the fallout.

THE RECKONING

So when my father died and we discovered there was nothing left, that decades of hard work and a good pension had all been gambled away, I understood why most of my siblings said no.

No, they wouldn't help pay for a private nursing home for our mother. No, they wouldn't contribute to the care she'd become accustomed to. No, they were done cleaning up the mess.

And I didn't judge them. I couldn't. They had given enough. Worried enough. Shown up enough. They had earned their "no."

But that left my mother in a situation she had never really faced: consequences.

My sisters and I did our best. We scrambled. We searched. We tried to find solutions. And that search led us to a whole new world I had never been exposed to: city-run nursing homes.

From comfortable living to necessities. Our tax money now paying for her care.

I wish I could tell you I felt clear about it all. But I didn't. I felt everything at once: anger at the choices they'd made, sadness for the woman who now had to live with those consequences, guilt that I couldn't fix it, relief that I didn't have to, shame for that part of me who thought she'd brought this on herself. The rollercoaster of emotions brought new meaning to the word "challenge." How in the world was I to see the *More* in this?

A WORLD I DIDN'T KNOW EXISTED

Walking into that first city-run facility was like stepping through a doorway into a reality I'd never had to face.

These weren't the places with fancy lobbies and activity coordinators and gardens. These were the places where people ended up when everything else had run out. Money. Options. Family willing to help. This was the safety net. And let me tell you, it's a net with a lot of holes.

I saw hallways that needed painting. Equipment that needed replacing. Rooms that felt more like survival than living. And I saw residents, so many residents, who seemed forgotten. Not by the staff, but by a system that had clearly forgotten them.

But here's what else I saw: caregivers who were trying their absolute best with almost nothing.

I watched them move from room to room, patient to patient, doing the work that most people don't want to do. Cleaning bodies. Changing adults who've lost their dignity along with their savings. Comforting people who are scared and confused and alone. And doing it all for wages that barely cover their own bills.

I saw the frustration in their eyes. The exhaustion. But I also saw the caring. The way they'd stop to hold a hand. The gentle way they'd speak to someone who wouldn't remember the conversation five minutes later. The extra moment they'd take to make sure someone was comfortable, even when they had ten other people waiting.

These people were heroes working in a system that treated them and the people they cared for like afterthoughts.

The underfunding was everywhere. Not enough staff. Not enough training. Not enough resources. Not enough time. Not enough respect. Not enough money to give people the basic dignity they deserved at the end of their lives.

And I kept thinking: How is this okay? How have we decided, as a society, that this is acceptable?

My mother had made terrible choices. But what about the woman in the room next to hers who'd done everything right? Who'd saved and planned but gotten cancer, and the treatments and inability to work bankrupted her? What about the people who'd worked their whole lives and simply outlived their savings?

Did they all deserve this bare-minimum existence?

THE AWAKENING

This experience cracked something open in me. It started me on a path of discovery I hadn't expected.

I began exploring other systemic failures. The homelessness crisis. The way we treat mental illness. The way we abandon people when they're most vulnerable.

And I saw the same pattern everywhere: not enough funding, not enough understanding, not enough respect for the people doing the frontline work, and not enough training to give them the tools they need to do it well.

These caregivers, whether they're working in city-run nursing homes or homeless shelters or crisis centers, they need *More*. *More* support. *More* training. *More* resources. *More* recognition that what they do matters. *More* money so they're not choosing between their own bills and showing up for one *more* shift.

And the people they care for? They need *More* too. *More* dignity. *More* options. *More* of a safety net that actually catches them. *More* of a society that sees them as human beings worthy of care, not just problems to warehouse until they die.

Years have passed since those darkest days. Time has a way of softening edges, of bringing clarity where there was once only chaos.

I visited my mother yesterday, and she was so much at peace. We talked, I brought her outside in her wheelchair, and we enjoyed watching squirrels and birds. I am able to love her and choose to see the abundance all around us.

BUT HERE'S WHAT LIVING IN *MORE* REALLY MEANS

This is what *More* looked like in the raw, unfiltered truth: it wasn't just about acknowledging what's broken. It was about having the faith to believe things could be different, the courage to look at what was needed, and the curiosity to discover what was already working.

Because here's what else I found:
people and organizations already
creating *More* in the midst of the lack.

I discovered Haven Toronto, the only Canadian organization dedicated exclusively to homeless men over 50, providing meals, crisis support, housing help, and dignity to a thousand clients at a time. I learned about Inner City Health Associates in Toronto, the largest homeless health organization in Canada, with physicians and nurses bringing medical care directly to people on the streets and in shelters.

I found HelpAge Canada, which works alongside community organizations to support older adults in aging with dignity. The Canadian Coalition for Seniors' Mental Health fights to ensure that the cause gets the recognition and resources it deserves.

And there were so many *more*, organizations I would never have known existed if I hadn't been forced to face the lack myself.

This is what *More* demands: not just a reality check, but the faith to believe solutions exist. The courage to acknowledge what's broken without becoming paralyzed by it. The curiosity to ask, "Who's already doing this work? How can I support them? What can I learn?"

I wouldn't have discovered any of this, wouldn't have seen the incredible people quietly changing lives every day, if my mother hadn't ended up in that city-run facility. If I hadn't been subjected to the lack, I never would have gone looking for the *more* that was already there, waiting to be found and supported.

Through those challenging years, I discovered a world of amazing caregivers who do the best they can with limited resources. I saw and still see the frustration in their eyes, as well as their caring intentions. I discovered that every moment is an opportunity to make someone else's life better.

I also learned the importance of asking: While you're looking for solutions and working toward what you want, whose life can you improve today?

The hard truth is this: **if you don't change something, nothing will change**.

"WHEN YOU SHIFT FROM
'WHY IS THIS HAPPENING
TO ME?' TO 'HOW CAN I
HELP SOMEONE ELSE
THROUGH THIS?', THAT'S
WHEN YOUR PAIN
TRANSFORMS INTO YOUR
PURPOSE."

– Denise Frenette

FROM AWAKENING TO ACTION

So here's what I learned through all of this: you can see the need for *More* in the world. You can understand it intellectually. You can even feel it in your bones. But none of that matters if you don't have daily practices that keep you aligned with it.

Because here's the truth: I couldn't have navigated those years with my mother, couldn't have seen the beauty in the caregivers, couldn't have discovered those organizations, couldn't have held both my anger and my compassion without the foundational practices that kept me grounded in *More* every single day.

These practices didn't make the hard things easy. But they made me strong enough to face them. Clear enough to see beyond them. Open enough to find meaning in them.

And how in the world was I able to still focus on what was good for me (my health, my career, my personal wants and dreams) while dealing with my mother's situation and the challenges it caused within my family? How did I not just survive it, but actually thrive through it?

The answer is in the daily practices. The small, consistent rituals that kept me grounded when everything else was chaos.

So if you're wondering, "Okay Denise, I get it. *More* is important. But how do I actually live it when life is kicking my ass?", here's how.

THE DAILY PRACTICE: YOUR MORNING *MORE* RITUAL

Here's a powerful yet simple transformational morning routine that, done consistently, will create a shift that brings you *More*. But you've got to believe. You've got to understand with your heart, not necessarily your brain, that this works.

Step 1: Acknowledge the Source

First thing in the morning, when you open your eyes, say, "Good morning," out loud. This is your way to acknowledge that there's an energetic source around you, spirit guides, God, angels, whatever feels comfortable, and you choose to connect to it.

Step 2: Invite Joy

Before sitting up in bed, take a slow, deep breath in, slowly exhale, then smile. A gentle, beautiful smile. Even if you don't feel happy, even if it feels fake. With this smile, say aloud: "I invite joy into my life."

Step 3: Claim Your Day—Set an intention

Claim the day you will have, even if you don't think it will happen. Here are examples:

- "Today, I will have a productive day and feel amazing!"

- "Today, I will be gentle with myself and kind to those around me."

- "Today, I choose to be focused and find solutions."

- "Today, I will make a positive difference in someone's life."

Then go on with your day with curiosity.

Do this **EVERY MORNING**. No matter what. And see what happens.

I've shared this practice with so many clients over my thirty years in health and wellness, and I can tell you, the ones who commit to it, who do it even when they don't feel like it, are the ones who experience the most profound shifts. It's not magic (though it feels like it sometimes). It's about training your nervous system to expect goodness, priming your brain to notice opportunities, and aligning your energy with what you want to create.

The beautiful thing is, this practice works whether you're spiritual, religious, or completely skeptical. Your brain doesn't care what you believe; it responds to consistency and intention.

Think of your brain like a computer that's just starting up in the morning.

When you first wake up, your brain isn't instantly "online." It's still transitioning from sleep mode to awake mode. During these first few minutes, your brain waves are in the same frequencies you'd find during deep meditation or learning states.

Here's what's actually happening:

Your brain has a built-in filtering system called the Reticular Activating System. It's like your personal assistant that decides what's important enough for you to notice each day. When you're waking up, this system is literally coming online and getting programmed for the day ahead.

So here's the opportunity:

Instead of letting your phone, your worries, or random thoughts be the first thing to program this system, you get to consciously choose what goes in first. When you speak to your spirit guide, read your affirmations, or set intentions in those first five minutes, you're essentially giving your brain's filtering system its marching orders.

Why this works:

Throughout the day, your brain will be unconsciously looking for evidence that matches whatever programming you gave it that morning. Set an intention for abundance? Your brain starts noticing opportunities. Affirm your strength? You'll catch yourself handling challenges better.

The bottom line: Your brain is going to get programmed anyway in those first few minutes, either by accident or on purpose. Why not take charge of that programming and point your mental filtering system toward what you actually want to experience?

I'm telling you, this practice didn't just help me get through those years after my father's death. It helped me see through different lenses. It gave me the ability to see those caregivers' frustrations not as failures, but as human beings doing the best they could with the tools they were given. It helped me move forward with grace rather than staying stuck in anger.

That's why I'm sharing this with you. Life can get pretty interesting at times. And it's absolutely incredible what becomes possible when we're able to see past the darkness.

THE SCIENCE BEHIND THE MAGIC

Now, I know some of you might be thinking, "Denise, this sounds a little too good to be true." And I get it. But stick with me here. Even if science isn't your thing, this information will help you understand why I do what I do—why, as a Transformational Life Coach, I take the time to show people different ways to connect on a deeper level.

Here's the simple truth: your brain has billions of neurons constantly communicating through electrical currents. When they fire together, they create waves, like ripples in water. And different types of waves create different states of being.

Scientists have identified five main types of brain waves: Delta (deep sleep and healing), Theta (meditation, creativity, and intuition), Alpha (relaxed awareness, perfect for visualization), Beta (active thinking and problem solving), and Gamma (peak mental states and heightened perception).

When you're stressed and overthinking? Your brain is firing in Beta. When you're meditating or setting intentions in that calm morning space? You're in Alpha and Theta. When you're in deep sleep or healing? That's Delta.

Here's why this matters: your brain waves in those first few minutes after waking are in the same frequencies you'd find during deep meditation or prayer: that Alpha and Theta zone. It's like your brain is in this magical, receptive state where it's most open to being programmed.

And here's the kicker about music: research shows that listening to somber, heavy music actually changes your brain chemistry in one direction, while uplifting, motivational music changes it in the opposite direction. Different frequencies stimulate the release of different neurotransmitters and hormones. Clinical trials have proven that specific sound frequencies can decrease anxiety and support emotional regulation.

That's right, hunny, listening to loud motivational music can literally change your brain chemistry and your life!

This is why your morning intention-setting works. You're not just thinking positive thoughts. You're literally training your brain to activate the areas associated with positivity and hope. **You're giving your brain's filtering system, the part that decides what's important enough for you to notice each day, its marching orders.**

So when I teach you to speak intentions out loud, to use music, to connect with source energy, I'm not just sharing spiritual woo-woo. I'm giving you scientifically backed tools to literally reshape your brain's electrical activity and, consequently, your reality.

> **Your thoughts truly do transform your life. When you choose thoughts of *More*, *more* love, *more* possibility, *more* solutions, you're tuning into frequencies that create those realities.**

The "how" of *More* isn't about hustling harder. It's about shifting how you move through the world. Here's what that actually looks like:

TRUST DEEPER

This doesn't mean blind faith or pretending everything's fine. It means trusting that you're being guided even when you can't see the full path. When I was navigating my mother's situation, I didn't know how it would all work out. But I trusted that each step would reveal the next one. And it did. Every single time.

Trust is a practice.
Start small.
Trust that the right conversation will happen.
Trust that the solution will appear.
Trust that you're exactly where you need to be, even when it feels like chaos.

QUESTION SMARTER

The questions you ask yourself shape your reality. Seriously. Your brain is designed to answer whatever question you give it, so if you're asking, "Why does this always happen to me?" your brain will find evidence that you're cursed. But if you ask, "What can I learn from this?" or "How can I grow through this?", your brain starts searching for possibilities instead of problems.

ASK BETTER QUESTIONS

Instead of "Why is this so hard?", ask, "How can I do this differently?"

Instead of "Why can't I figure this out?", ask, "What's one small step I can take today?"

Instead of "Why doesn't anything ever work for me?", ask, "What's working that I haven't noticed yet?"

The shift from "why me?" to "what now?"
is the difference between staying stuck
and moving forward.

SURRENDER THE IDEA THAT YOU HAVE TO DO IT ALL ALONE

This one's hard, especially if you've been the strong one, the fixer, the person everyone else leans on. But here's the truth: you were never meant to carry it all by yourself.

Ask for help. From people. From the Universe. From your spirit guides. From that friend who keeps offering. From professionals who know what you don't.

I couldn't have navigated those years with my mother alone. I needed my sisters. I needed the social workers. I needed those caregivers. I needed my morning practice connecting to something bigger than myself. And I needed to be okay with needing all of that.

Surrendering isn't giving up. It's recognizing that collaboration, with people and with the Universe, is how we create *More*. Not through force, but through flow.

REDEFINE COURAGE

Courage isn't the absence of fear—it's doing it scared. The smallest step in the right direction can change your life forever.

Sometimes courage feels anything but comfortable. It rattles the heart. It asks us to risk reputation, and sometimes even life itself. But courage is also the language of the Universe. It's the moment when we say, "I trust there's *more* guiding me than what I can see right now."

History keeps reminding us of this. Small refusals, whispered truths, and steady resistance have shaped entire societies. One choice. One voice. One step. That's all it takes to send ripples through time.

Think of Rosa Parks on that bus. She wasn't loud. She wasn't carrying a sign. She simply stayed in her seat. But that quiet act shook the walls of injustice and carried forward a movement that changed millions of lives. That's the power of courage. It doesn't shout; it simply refuses to back down.

And when we choose courage, we're never moving alone. The energy of the Universe stands with us when we dare to move forward, even trembling.

THAT'S THE CONNECTION.
THAT'S THE REMINDER.

Universal energy doesn't push us into comfort; it invites us into alignment. It whispers, you're held, you're guided, now step. And when you listen to that whisper, your courage becomes the bridge between fear and freedom.

UPGRADE YOUR PERCEPTION

Old story: "I'm stuck." New story: "I'm being prepared for something bigger."

You were built for *More*. Not just crumbs. Not just survival. A feast.

And the beautiful truth? You don't have to wait for perfect conditions. You can start right now, right where you are, with what you have.

BECAUSE *MORE* ISN'T SOMETHING YOU
FIND. IT'S SOMETHING YOU BECOME.

Now that you're starting to get a clearer picture of what *More* truly is and how to begin embodying it daily, you're probably wondering: "But when? When is the right time to make these changes? When do I finally stop waiting and start living?" That's exactly where we're going next. Because timing, my friend, is everything, and nothing, all at once.

"YOUR VISION OF MORE ISN'T TOO BIG FOR THIS WORLD. LET ITS PURPOSE BRING FREEDOM TO WHAT HAS NOT BEEN QUESTIONED YET."

— Denise Frenette

PART 4: WHEN

WHEN DO WE START?

The Time Is Now

The Time for *More*

Here's what I know about timing: it's never perfect. It's never convenient. And it's never going to feel "right."

But here's what else I know: every single person who has ever created something meaningful, who has ever broken a cycle, who has ever chosen *More*—they all started on a day that felt like any other day.

They started scared.

They started imperfect.

And, they started anyway.

So, let's do something right now. Together.

I want you to handwrite what I've written in the next few **pages**. Copy it as you see it. Capital letters and all.

And then, read it out loud and share with me how it made you feel. Did it make you feel silly? Even if no one was looking? Did it make you feel like this was not you? Did it make you feel empowered?

I want you to do this for real. Ok?

Here we go:

I
AM
LOVED

Your turn:

_____

_____

_____

Keep going:

I
AM
WORTHY

Come on, you can do it.

_____

_____

_____

You know the drill:

I
AM
FORGIVING

Just do it already.

_____

_____

_____

Last one:

I
AM
BEAUTIFUL

And, that you are!

_____

_____

_____

WAIT A MINUTE...
DID YOU READ IT OUT LOUD?

If not, go back and **do it...** and if not out loud, then simply whisper those powerful words of affirmation.

So, I wonder, when you heard your voice speak these affirmations, how did it make **you** feel?

Here's why I had you do that. Whatever you felt, whether it was silly, empowering, uncomfortable, or transformative, your body just experienced a shift in frequency. And **that** shift? It's not just happening inside you. It's rippling out into everything around you.

Remember what I told you earlier about brainwaves and how your thoughts literally change your brain's electrical activity? Well, it goes deeper than that. Every single thing you experience, everything you hear, everything you see, everything you smell, and everything you think creates your perceived reality. But here's **the** part that will blow your mind: your frequency doesn't just stay contained in your head. It changes your environment.

When you wrote those words, when you spoke them out loud, you didn't just change your thoughts. You changed the electromagnetic field around your body. You **shifted** the vibration you're putting out into the world. And the world responds to that.

Think about it: Have you ever walked into a room and immediately felt the "vibe"? That's not just metaphorical, that's measurable energy. When someone is angry, you can feel it before they even speak. When someone is genuinely joyful, it's contagious. When someone is operating from a place of love and abundance, people are drawn to them like a magnet.

THAT'S YOUR FREQUENCY AT WORK.

When you declared, "I AM LOVED," whether you believed it or not, whether it felt true or foreign, you sent a signal out into the Universe. You told the quantum field around you, "This is who I am. This is what I'm claiming." And the Universe, in all its mysterious ways, starts rearranging itself to match that frequency.

This isn't wishful thinking. This is science meeting spirit. Your thoughts create neural pathways. Your emotions release hormones. Your intentions shift your energy field. And that energy field interacts with everything and everyone around you.

And here's the thing: even if you don't believe in what you're reading right now, even if you don't feel it at first, the *more* you let your eyes see those words, the *more* your ears hear those words spoken about you, the *more* it registers in your brain. And then, it becomes you.

Just like the son who hears his father telling him to "smarten up" all the time becomes anxious and self-doubting. Just like the boy who lives in fear all the time learns that the world is dangerous. Just like the child who sees violence learns that aggression is normal. All these things shape us whether we like it or not. Our brains don't ask permission, they just absorb and adapt.

But here's the beautiful part: if negative patterns can **shape** who you are, so can positive ones. You can now reshape who you are deliberately. **These habits, these thoughts, these words, transform your world.**

So choose wisely.

Do you want to create and experience a world that puts you down and limits you?

Or do you want to live in a world that says:

I AM CAPABLE

I AM BEAUTIFUL

I AM WORTHY

I AM INTELLIGENT

I AM SAFE

I AM LOVED

You choose. Every single day, with every thought you think, every word you speak to yourself, **every** image you let settle into your mind... You choose. And that choice doesn't just change you. It changes everything around you.

So when I ask you about timing, when the right time is to start living *more*, I'm really asking: **When** are you ready to change your frequency? And when are you going to **choose** to see things differently?

BECAUSE THE MOMENT YOU DO,

EVERYTHING STARTS SHIFTING.

Not just inside you, **but** around you. Your relationships. Your opportunities. Your entire experience of life.

The person who writes "I AM LOVED" and means it shows up differently in the world from the person who believes they must earn love through suffering. The man who claims his worth doesn't wait for permission to pursue his dreams. The person operating from abundance attracts abundance, not because they're magical, but because they're **broadcasting** a different signal.

This is why the timing is always now. **Your frequency is always broadcasting.** The question isn't whether you're ready for everything to be perfect; it's whether you're ready to start sending out a signal that matches what you want to create.

THE DAY I STOPPED WAITING FOR PERMISSION

Let me tell you about the moment I realized that waiting for the "right time" was just another way of staying small.

For years, I carried stories inside me... stories of dysfunction, fear, and pain. I stayed silent because:

What if people judge me? What if my truth ruins the "perfect family" illusion? What if I'm not strong enough to handle the consequences?

But here's what happened instead: the silence started killing me.

Resentment grew.

Anger festered.

And I realized that keeping quiet wasn't protecting anyone. It was just keeping us all stuck in the same painful patterns.

SO I FACED MY FEAR.

I WROTE.

I SPOKE.

NOT TO SHAME, BUT TO FREE.

NOT TO EXPOSE, BUT TO HEAL.

And something miraculous happened: the shame **that** had lived in me for generations finally had a place to go. The weight I'd been carrying began to lift.

And me? I finally breathed.

"YOUR VOICE BECOMES POWERFUL THE MOMENT YOU USE IT NOT JUST FOR YOURSELF, BUT FOR SOMEONE WHO'S BEEN SILENCED. LOVE DOESN'T WHISPER WHEN JUSTICE IS NEEDED."

– *Denise Frenette*

WHEN LOVE DEMANDS ACTION

I didn't break my silence for fame. Or revenge. Or even "healing."

I did it for my son. For my stepdaughter. For my husband, John. For the little versions of my siblings and me who deserved better. For all those who are suppressed and silenced by unhealed anger.

I did it because love doesn't stay silent when it sees suffering.

Love says: We can have *more*. We deserve *more*. And it's time things change.

And that's when I understood: the "when" isn't about perfect timing. It's about courage. **And accountability**. The courage to break cycles instead of perpetuating them, **and the accountability to keep showing up even when it's hard, even when you don't feel like it, even when the change feels impossible.** The courage to choose healing over hiding. The courage to believe that your story, messy, imperfect, real, might be exactly what someone else needs to hear.

But courage alone isn't enough. You also need to keep **showing up**.

THE MOMENT EVERYTHING CLICKS

There's a moment that comes when you've been living in the essence of *More* for a while. It's subtle at first, then unmistakable.

You stop asking, "When will things get better?" and start noticing that they already are.

> **You stop waiting for other people to change and realize you've become the change.**

You stop searching for *More* and recognize you've been living it all along.

For me, that moment came during a recent visit with my mother, the same woman whose financial crisis had once filled me with rage and shame. There she was, in her wheelchair in a city-run nursing home, watching squirrels with the wonder of a child.

And I felt... grateful. Not for her circumstances, but for her peace. For the incredible staff who care for her. For the system that, however imperfect, ensures that she's safe. For my own ability to see abundance where I once saw only lack.

That's when I knew: *More* isn't something you achieve. It's something you become.

"TRUST ISN'T BELIEVING EVERYTHING WILL WORK OUT PERFECTLY. IT'S KNOWING YOU'LL FIND YOUR WAY THROUGH WHATEVER COMES."

– Denise Frenette

YOUR TIME IS NOW

As Chris Hedges said: "Hope is not about the right attitude. Hope is not about peace of mind. Hope is action. Hope is doing something."

You are standing at the edge of *More* right now.

More **freedom** from the stories that have kept you small.

More **love** than you ever thought possible.

More **impact** than you dare to imagine.

And what you do today, this moment, this breath, determines your *More*.

NOT TOMORROW WHEN YOU FEEL BRAVER.

NOT NEXT WEEK WHEN LIFE CALMS DOWN.

NOT SOMEDAY WHEN THE STARS ALIGN.

NOW

THE WORLD THAT'S WAITING

I want you in my world.
In my world of More.

A world that **celebrates** all shades of colors. A world that protects, that embraces what is different, that is inclusive in all dimensions, and a world that respects all living things.

A world that **allows** for both five-star restaurants and safe places for children to dream.

A world that **invites** creativity and beauty AND fosters healing spaces for wounded souls.

A world that **wants** you to change the way you think, the way you see others, and the way you see yourself.

A world that **explores** every curiosity while understanding the unlimited power that lies beyond our perceived limitations. Beyond our fears. Beyond even our biggest visions.

This world already exists. We're building it every day, each time we choose compassion over judgment, hope over resignation, abundance over greed, action over waiting.

YOUR NEXT MOVE

Don't wait for a sign. This is your sign.

Don't wait for courage. Courage comes from doing it scared.

Don't wait for *more* time, *more* money, *more* anything.

You have everything you need right now to take one step towards *More*.

So here's my invitation:

Demand *More*. Not just for yourself, but for everyone whose life you touch.

Claim your essence.

You are worthy.

You are not too much.

You are exactly who this world needs.

Dare to discover. The *More* in who you are.
The *More* in what surrounds us all.

The door to *More* isn't just open. You're already standing in the doorway.

All that's left is to step through.

And when you do, when you finally claim your *More*, you'll realize something beautiful:

You weren't just seeking *More*.

***More* was seeking you.**

It always has been.

Welcome home.

With endless love and possibility,

Denise

...WAIT A MINUTE! ONE LAST THING. ⟶

A LITTLE SOMETHING
BEFORE YOU GO...

Hey there, beautiful human who just finished reading my book!

FIRST OFF, YOU'RE AMAZING.

Seriously. You took time out of your busy, probably slightly chaotic life to read about MORE, and that means the world to me.

Now, I have a tiny, itsy-bitsy favor to ask. You know how, when you finish a great meal at a restaurant, the server asks if everything was okay? Well, this is kind of like that, except I can't see your face or hear your answer (which is probably for the best because I'd be nervously rambling right now).

If this book gave you even a little spark of inspiration, made you smile, or helped you find your own MORE, would you mind hopping over to Amazon and leaving a review? And here's the thing, I'm not asking for five stars if you didn't love it. I'm asking for your honest thoughts.

But if you DID love it... well, five stars would make me do a happy dance in my kitchen. Just saying.

Scan here to leave a review. (Your future self will thank you for this good karma.)

ACKNOWLEDGMENTS

First and foremost, thank you to my husband, **John**, who has encouraged me in ways I can't even begin to express. Your unwavering support made this dream possible.

To **YOU.** The resilient, gentle, funny, and beautiful soul who helped me when I was alone. Who didn't judge. Who smiled. YOU KNOW WHO YOU ARE. xo

To all of my **clients** who continue to give me purpose and value, this book exists because of the trust you place in me and the lessons we discover together.

My heartfelt gratitude goes to my **sisters** and **brothers**, whose love and connection have shaped who I am today.

To my **parents**, thank you for doing the best you could with what you were given. Even imperfect love teaches us something valuable about MORE.

A big THANK YOU to the amazing Amelie Valois for her incredible, creative design expertise. To Anna Odeh Photography for your extraordinary talent, and let's not forget Ellie Laliberté, Penny Dawson, and Lucky Book Publishing. You have helped bring my MORE to fruition..

For those who took the time to read my manuscript and share your insights (you know who you are), your feedback was invaluable in making this book what it became.

And finally, to myself, for having the courage to write the words that needed to be written.

To everyone who finds MORE in these pages, this journey continues because of all of you.

ABOUT THE AUTHOR

DENISE FRENETTE is a mom, wife, (ex-wife), daughter, sister, and woman who believes in *MORE*. She is a Spiritual Synergist and Transformational Life Coach who has spent over twenty-five years helping people break through the patterns that keep them stuck.

After growing up in a strict Catholic household where appearances mattered more than truth, she learned firsthand the cost of making herself smaller to fit others' expectations. For years, she hid her intuitive and mediumship abilities, afraid of judgment. But when life brought her to a breaking point, she made a radical choice: to stop hiding and start living authentically.

Today, Denise works at the intersection of practical transformation and spiritual insight, helping clients see the energetic patterns running their lives and giving them concrete tools to rewrite those patterns. She believes that when we shift our perception and connect to universal energy, we create a ripple effect that touches everyone around us.

Her greatest passions are her amazing son, incredible stepdaughter, and husband (the same one she almost left but chose to love differently). She continues having daily conversations with spirit guides while blasting motivational music, and loves traveling, exploring friendly pubs, meeting people from different walks of life, and discovering five-star restaurants.

To learn more visit www.denisefrenette.com/book.

MORE ... Because It's Time is her first book, born from a four-year journey to find the right words to share what she's learned about transformation, worthiness, and the revolutionary act of wanting *More*.